Out of a Land of Alkali & Chromate is about coming from, going out, and finding home. Growing up with an unpredictable and violent father, Landgraf found sanctuary with her grandparents and in books, food, and fairy tales. This is a story of yearning and seeking—both with some help from a prince and in the many other ways she found possible to make a life of her own.

"In Susan Landgraf's *Out of a Land of Alkali & Chromate*, time arcs wide as we take a poetic journey by train from childhood trauma woven with wonder and ancestral legends to a new land of brave introspection and joy. Landgraf's matter-of-fact voice brings difficult subjects to the forefront in a way that is both charming and arresting. Untold fairy tale backstories come to light in this collection and expand the meanings of these engaging poems."

—Katy E. Ellis, author of
Forty Bouts in the Wilderness

OUT OF A LAND OF ALKALI & CHROMATE

OUT OF A LAND OF ALKALI & CHROMATE

Susan Landgraf

MoonPath Press

Copyright © 2025 Susan Landgraf
All rights reserved.

No part of this publication may be reproduced, distributed, or transmitted in any form or by any means whatsoever without written permission from the publisher, except in the case of brief excerpts for critical reviews and articles. All inquiries should be addressed to MoonPath Press.

Poetry
ISBN 979-8-9899487-4-1

Cover art: *Alkali and Chromate*, 2024, mixed media
by Gabriela Denise Frank
GabrielaDeniseFrank.com

Author photo: Tim Aguero

Book design by Tonya Namura, using BD Supper (display)
and Gentium Book Basic (text)

MoonPath Press, an imprint of Concrete Wolf Poetry Series,
is dedicated to publishing the finest poets
living in the U.S. Pacific Northwest.

MoonPath Press
c/o Concrete Wolf
PO Box 2220
Newport, OR 97365-0163

MoonPathPress@gmail.com

http://MoonPathPress.com

*For my family, friends, and teachers—
all of you who have given me support, ideas,
blessings, and love;
and especially my children,
Brett Landgraf, Ted Landgraf, Jennifer Landgraf,
and Lisa Nichols.*

CONTENTS

I — BEGINNING

Family Tree on My Mother's Side, Painesville, Ohio, USA
   * Why Some Hungarians Dream Equations and Notes, 5
   * Sunflowers, 6
   * ....mystics of the world speak the same language, 7

My Mother's Birth, 8

My Grandmother's Hungarian Horns and Sunday Dinner, 9

Getting Ready for Christ, 10

The Cemetery Again, 11

Snake, 13

Two Photos
   1. No names on the back, only the black-and-white, 15
   2. The house built out of a chicken coop sits in a field., 16

...all the king's horses and all the king's men..., 17

Woodshed, 18

Lunch Break in the Berry Field at Champion's Nursery, 19

Under Heaven, 20

II — INTERIM

Bleach, 23

Rampion, the Beautiful, 24

Rapunzel Writes a Letter to the Editor, 26

Into Straw Out of Oz, 27

Old Shoe Woman Who Wasn't There in the 1930s Print, 28

Without Towers or Wands, 30

Note I Pinned to a Tree for Red Riding Hood's Mother
at the Edge of the Woods Where She Will Be Sure
to Find It, 32

Why Didn't the Princess's Mother Tell the King
to Stick It Up His Kingdom?, 34

Feather Leaf Tree, 36

Tree Temple, 37

III — LEAVINGS

Crossings, 43

The Way I Came Out of the Cellar, 44

Saving, 45

Finding My Grandmother's Childhood Home,
Öskü, Hungary, 46

My Cinderella Story, 47

Miscarriage, 49

Land of Alkali and Chromate, 50

Having Been Born in Painesville, 51

Canned Peaches, 52

Written Affair, 53

General Note Written to Anyone Who Might Chance to
Discover One of My Lost Tupperware Bowls,
That Stage of My Life Happening to Be Over, 54

Semi-Sonata of Oranges, 55

Original Sin on the Road, 56

The Yolk and the White of It, 57

IV — AFTER

Wolf, I Remember You, 61

Art of Conjugating *To Desire*, 62

Rainier, 63

Altars, 65

The Ten Stations of Worship, 66

Afternoon Affair, 67

Eight Notes to Some of You Who Make Me Happy
    Dear Garlic, 68
    Artichokes, 69
    Cabbage, 70
    Oh, My Beloved Potatoes, 71
    Hello, Cheetos, 72
    Pomegranate, 73
    To You, Oysters, That Gave Me 12 Ways to Pray, 74
    Meditation with Peach, 76

Bindweed, 77

Places That Made Me, 78

Recipe for Making a Day, 79

Two Letters
    1. To My Martian and Hungarian Ancestors, 80
    2. Reminders to Self, 81

NOTES, 83

ACKNOWLEDGEMENTS, 87

GRATITUDE, 89

ABOUT THE ARTIST, 91

ABOUT THE AUTHOR, 93

OUT OF A LAND OF ALKALI & CHROMATE

I — BEGINNING

I heard trains before I saw them, woke to whistles
in the middle of the night crossing Bowhall Road,
shaking my iron bed. I lay tucked between the covers
as they sped to somewhere glamorous—
like Las Vegas.

In the glider swing on my grandmother's porch I played
engineer—two pushes to Cleveland in command of that
huge beast
with its one bright eye, pistons, wheels, and its bellied fire.
Boxcars coupled, their wheels sparked the rails.

Muscled, fast, complete worlds unto themselves like the
Roma
caravans my grandmother remembered but fast, faster past
cornfields, towns, through mountains and cities, complete
with draft gears, cooling systems, valve covers, and axles.

Family Tree on My Mother's Side, Painesville, Ohio, USA

*

Why Some Hungarians Dream Equations and Notes

More musicians and mathematicians
than anywhere else—too many Martians, not enough
spaceships to take them back—the sudden exodus
like a great flock of herons
slipping through a blue lip in the sky.

The Roma women's skirts unfurled
to red and purple flowers, the men's voices
reverberated like echoes
in a well. Their stories
flickered around the campfire: how the abandoned

pocketed themselves from the sea and the moon's pull,
whirled like a compass needle
in the dark. They used scales as metaphors.
Their long-handled cups held the moon.
They mixed with the natives.

Finding blue bloods now would be hard as going home
without a ship—but a thread holds
the magnetic resonance in their equations,
their songs throbbing
with a blue planetary hum.

*
Sunflowers

They grow for their own sake in that land
of Bartók's folk songs, full-blooded and rich.
That land where *common revolutionaries
take action.* That land of peasants and mystics
and sunflowers, here now in Ohio growing
in my grandmother's garden, each on its one
stout leg, faces following the sun the same
as in the old country, these flowers asking
for nothing but sun and rain and, yes, adoration.

*

*...mystics of the world speak the same
language*
        Meister Eckhart

She could be the copper girl, a seeker
across the steppes in a wagon where
a conqueror's thundering hoofbeats
sent her across the sea. She listened
        to wind-rustled mulberry
        the sun god's light locked
        inside, the inner altar's great stones
        blessed by Neptune and Jupiter,
        by spider, grape vines, lightning
and she heard the birthings
                          that hum—

My Mother's Birth

My grandmother's body shuddered
like a house in a storm, shutters loose, banging
her ribs. This was July and she was alone,
this baby wanting to come too soon.
        She wanted to be out staking the peas.
        God was napping under a tree.
She wrapped white flannel strips around
fingers without nails, legs like chicken
legs and toes like peas picked too early.
Nestled the child like half a loaf of bread
        in a shoebox lined with boiled rags. Slid
        the box into the cookstove warming oven.
She dreamed her apron full of tender
green globes, woke to a bird's cry, lifted
her daughter light as a canary's wishbone
and willed her to hold. She remembered God
        napping under a tree. She'd been tempted
        to hit him over the head with her hoe.

My Grandmother's Hungarian Horns and
Sunday Dinner

She leaned over the Formica kitchen table, stretched
dough thinner than skin, her breasts squashed against
the cold metal edge. She had practiced her English:
one-half pound vaj—nem—butter, 3 egg yolks,
2 cups flour, one-half korsó—nem—pint of sour cream.
After she knifed the dough, spread poppy seed paste
and pinched each horn together same as her mother
in the old country, she turned the oven on, marveled
at this magic of electricity her mother never had.

Mid-morning she lifted the oldest hen, ringed
its neck with her left hand, circled the axe handle
with her right. *I have an axe. I kill the chicken.*
She pictured the new words she was learning as she waited,
apron splattered with blood, until the headless chicken
stopped dancing in the red-tipped grass. Then she headed
to the kitchen with its pot of boiling water for what
she hated most—*toll kopasztás*—the feather plucking.
What words would she use to explain this in English.

Getting Ready for Christ

She carted everything out from under the eaves—
yellowed wedding dress with its hundred buttons, photos,
a box of never-worn baby clothes. She scrubbed the floor
on her hands and knees. Put it all back.

She sorted her clothes—one pile for the church, another
to ship overseas to my grandfather's family, the rest back
into drawers and closets in perfect rows, like the carrots
and potatoes already planted in the garden.

In my room she dusted Jesus, framed behind glass holding
his bleeding heart in his hands over my bed. Downstairs
more dusting and sweeping. Then the windows and oven.
Finally the basement with its coal bin,

washtubs, and two-bucket wine press. On Easter morning
we wore our new hats and shoes to church; came home
to baked ham, kiffles, and poppy seed kolache.
Take, eat... A quarter inch

of my grandfather's wine. *Take, drink...* And Christ?
Out of his tomb but still hanging over my bed
in this immaculate house
of resurrection.

The Cemetery Again

I didn't want to dress in my snow pants, jacket, boots,
muffler, and hat to go pick up my father. *He said he was
sorry*, my mother said, as she scooted the three of us up
the stairs out of the basement where we lived
into the snowy night. I scrunched into the car seat.

Sharon whimpered, *I'm cold. Crybaby*, I said. *Shhh*,
mother said. *Well, it's cold*, Linda said, her teeth chattering.

Mother fiddled with the heater knob, bent to see around the
flip-flapping windshield wipers. *Where are we going*, we
chorused in the dark car on the snow-covered road.
She leaned further into the steering wheel. *Front gate
at the cemetery*, she said.

I knew dead people couldn't see out of their graves.
Maybe they'd gone to heaven, at least some of them,
like my grandmother said, and that's how they could do it—
watch from their graves even when they were covered
with dirt. Maybe all dead people turned into magicians,
like the one I saw make scarves disappear, a rabbit
pop out of a hat.

Why's he waiting there? Linda asked. Sharon had fallen
asleep, her head cocked to the side like her rag doll.
It was okay to fall asleep when you were only four.

The snow fell harder, flakes looking like white needles
slicing the Studebaker's yellow light beams. We were
alone on the road. *He was crying*, mother said.

Why bury people if they're dead? Why a fence?

A cold blast blew in when the door opened. My father slammed it shut. I scrunched down into my coat. I thought about how the sheets in my bed would feel like ice.

S   a   k
    n   e

After I learned the words
slither & Satan

I was afraid
to touch the page with
S   a   k
    n   e
in my alphabet book

      Eve wanted words   what she got
      was birth.

      I learned that later.

My father dug the foundation
for our house—
    brick & stone
    cherry & pine
    shouts & bruises—

found
a black
S   a   k
    n   e
used the shovel blade, pitched me
    the halves.

Two
S   a
    n
                    k   e   s
twitched at my feet
            I screamed.
            He laughed.

Two Photos

1.

No names on the back, only the black-and-white
babushka-covered heads, cow off to the left
a dusty tree, sepia sky

       the Hungarian plains always ripe
       for the picking but no planes
       in this photo between wars

              my grandmother saying
              as she taped up the box of food
              and clothes to take to the post office

                     they have nothing

2.

The house built out of a chicken coop sits in a field.
My sisters and I squint in the early afternoon sun.
My father is bald.

I want to pick dandelions, hundreds growing like fallen
suns in the grass. I haven't learned yet
they're called weeds. I want to pick a bouquet

to give my mother. She holds
a camera; she's a shadow in the glare.
My father is the only one smiling.

After my sisters and I go to bed, I listen to him
scrape his chair close to the radio. The creaking door opens
to *The Inner Sanctum* and the host's

disembodied voice: *I'm glad you came tonight, because
we have a very special guest of horror...*
I pull the quilt up to my chin

and hear the dandelions: *Remember us holding
the sun in our faces. Pick a bouquet
before your father mows us down.*

...all the king's horses and all the king's men...

My sisters and I dye eggs, pile
them in the crockery bowl as if they are golden.
New patent shoes wait under our beds
for the next day's resurrection.

If she wasn't good enough for him...
my father says before the gun's sharp retort crackles
like an egg in the enameled pan.
My mother ducks...

He fires again. When he gets
out of the hospital, bandages turban his head
like a white upside-down egg cup...
We visit him on the weekends

learning to hide our bruises
growing out of our new shoes.

Woodshed

the outside latch clicks closed and I hear

s   i   er
    l   th
                                                              ing

in the dark

        smells of wood   not fire

the devil does not hold
      a pitchfork   he has no hands

he does not speak
                but I hear a whisper
                maybe a squeak

the lock being lifted
                          my grandmother
holds me

Lunch Break in the Strawberry Field at Champion's Nursery

My father had forbidden my mother and grandmother to talk *that foreign tongue*. Hadn't my mother *flunked first grade for Christ's sake* because she spoke only Hungarian?

I had passed third grade, learned how letters looped, dipped, and rolled. I liked the way sun flooded my grandparent's porch, the *dichotomy*—that was a new word—of sun and flood. I tasted words:

> *dichotomy* was tapioca pudding,
> *sun* meant peaches,
> *flood* was burned, brittle caramel.

Strawberries were like words—some more juicy than others, some more tart. When I plucked a berry and put it to my lips, my grandmother said, *Ne. But one couldn't hurt.* I savored that first bite into its silky belly. My throat swirled.

By lunch I was soaked with sweat. I ate the cold cabbage soup Gram had packed in the Mason jar. I stretched out under the oak tree's shade and listened to words like muted colors I couldn't understand. I thought I would never be able to forgive my father.

Years later I look up a few Hungarian words I never learned to speak.
> Strawberry is *eper*,
> Grandmother is *nagymama*,
> and I have forgiven my *apa*.

Under Heaven

After the priest breathes amen over our grandmother,
        who saved the best plums, tomatoes, and hope
        in years leaning heavy on survival and weep;
        who told us, her granddaughters, make believe
        was better than fancy,
                something kept two of the three
        of us alive. Perhaps it was the chicken soup, soap
        ends, or string, the piggy bank with a hundred dimes
        or the rocking chair with its broken back.
        Occasionally, a ghost set it to creaking, some
        comfort in the world of lost souls.
                For the dead sister
        we could do nothing, neither invent a future
        free of tribulations nor the past. Stories had helped,
        grandmother's hand cooling our fevered brows,
        and maybe Christ with his enlarged red heart
        and golden crown over our beds watching.
                Or it was simply fate,
        a worm choosing one fruit over another,
        one rose bush growing only thorns.
                Meanwhile,
our grandmother lies in her plot, her allotted ground space
unkept by the younger generation
who have chosen not to save, forever, her death.

II — INTERIM

I imagined the boxcars as they came round the bend—
a snake uncoiling, carrying grain, lumber, coal, and meat.
Hoboes, too. Like the ones that camped under the huge oak
down by the Dairy Queen. I was forbidden to say *hello*

when we walked by. But I snuck a look. Two, three, four
crouched on stumps or the ground drinking coffee from tin
cups, the pot balanced over a small fire. I pictured them
hurling duffel bags into the open door of a moving car and
leaping.

I pictured me sitting in the dining car, silverware on a white
tablecloth, linen napkins, gleaming silverware. I'd heard
stories, seen pictures. On the glider swing four pushes to
Chicago. Injectors, flywheels, throttles,
brakes.

One day my father slammed on the brakes just before the
tracks, got out, cut a willow. The branch tracked my
buttocks and the backs of my legs. No conductor
as witness—only my mother. Five pushes to Florida…

Bleach

Hey, you, afraid of losing
your edge
afraid you'll get lost
in that big box
of discards
here's the deal
convince
others to stay between
the lines
like loyal soldiers
to green grass
to blue sky
whiten up the skin tones
and repeat after me
There are no purple pumpkins.

Rampion, the Beautiful

1.
No wonder Rapunzel's mother wanted
what was fresh, green, and obvious
in the middle of the witch's forbidden
garden, a woman pregnant with unusual
cravings but having such bad taste
in neighbors.

          Ah, the witch—
      now there was a schemer, thorns
      and shears in hand on cue, not to mention
      a tower with neither staircase nor door.

No one asked how the witch climbed
before Rapunzel's hair grew 20 ells,
a girl with shimmering hair
and inherited hunger that could
stop a king's son in his tracks.

          Imagine
      being the first man a girl had ever seen,
      nothing to compare to except the witch, who
      may or may not have been ugly, but who liked
      to climb and coveted a calendar.
      What better way than being close to the turns
      of a young girl's blood?

The prince paid with his eyes, weeping
in the wilderness until he heard
his beloved sing. Did he never ask
after her innocence or question
what it took to be queen

                she in that tower
                all those years without embroidery
                or loom, no stashes of imagination to show.

2.
Some women would sell their jewels
for such privacy and quiet knowing,
perhaps, that the witch was lonely but open
to compromise.

                As for Rapunzel's mother,
                she had never learned consequence,
                while Rapunzel's father was an unknown—
                killed by wolves or dodging
                child support in the days before Freud.

3.
Of course, a tuber is a tuber but this one has class—
European bellflower growing fresh and green,
with the gift of reproduction,
with the power
to satisfy a woman's craving.

Rapunzel Writes a Letter to the Editor

Please set the facts straight.
The witch Dame Gothel loved my hair.
First, of course, she needed
to climb. But more than that
it was for pleasure. She had thin hair,
wirelike and beginning to gray.

Sometimes I wondered what she did
with her hands when she wasn't
brushing and plaiting my hair.
I was like a museum piece out there
in Idaho's no-man's-land. At least I think
that's where it was. I'm not good with maps.

And neither was the prince once he went blind.
As for bleeding, yes, I did like any young
woman. I wasn't afraid. Dame Gothel was.
I didn't kill her.
I bore twins—a boy and a girl.
I never went back to the tower.

Into Straw Out Of Oz

Straw to gold, then what?
The miller's daughter never asked
the good in any language when it blames.

    Of course writers layer with metaphor,
    wizards use smoke screens, and in Oz
    the scarecrow got a brain.

        Scarecrows prove the versatility
        of straw, good for bedding down,
        divining the way wind blows.

            History books keep caged mice
            wired with electrodes, Sioux's land
            restitched by guilt, showered Jews.

                I had fancied myself spinning
                all night into a golden flame
                or inventing a new truth

                    when here it was—
                    the full-bloomed truth:
                    In a storm one stalk can spear a fence post.

Old Shoe Woman Who Wasn't There in the 1930s Print

> *...gave them some broth*
> *without any bread*
> *and spanked them all soundly...*

Sky's as blue and smooth as a robin egg and it's clear the old woman doesn't live with tornadoes or fear of being reported to the authorities.

Obviously cheaper by the dozen, two dozen in fact, the children slide down the shoestrings of the eight-holed, two-storied high-top with a chimney. It's summer, and a goose wearing an apron and hat scrubs one of the rosy-cheeked children in a tub. Others leap out of one of the windows, one swings from a shutter. They're all bare-ass naked, wearing smiles big as soap bubbles floating in the cloudless background.

Perhaps the mother's off with a lover or having a martini at the local gin mill and by four or five will show up to give the children their broth, with or without help from the goose, who doesn't seem worried she could be on the menu for Thursday night's supper. Could be it's a Sunday—but how could one mother and a goose get twenty-four children ready to sit quietly in church pews?

But it's not only the mother who's missing. No chirps, no arguments over turns as the children pull each other up the shoe's tongue, no diving board twang, growling stomachs. Just a pastoralist's Mother Goose before the Second Great War, before Disney's remake of *La Belle et la Bête*—

just make-believe cheesy-cheeked
innocents who would not grow up

to be rapists, terrorists, or drunks, who wouldn't throw a
grenade or bomb a plaza, who couldn't envision the '40s,
who wouldn't cry out in the middle of their nightmares.

Without Towers or Wands

Years she searched for shoes that didn't chafe
or pinch, but she'd inherited
her grandfather's side. She would never learn
to walk softly or take mincing steps.

Limping on blisters and corns, she chanted
the happily-ever-after and resisted
the surgeon's advice to break her feet.
Sins of the father took on a new fit.

And though she massaged and manicured,
she knew no knight would ask to hold
her feet in his hands. One of those self-help
books explained: She was becoming the man

her mother had hoped she'd marry.
Fitting for the times, as the prince
had a bad case of hoof 'n' mouth and no
practice building alliances or organizing

the king's garbage collection. In fact,
the kingdom was going to hell
under a stamp of rhetoric and growing
defense. She knew pumpkins left

in the field went to crows and rats.
And a rat is a rat. An incompetent prince
was as likely to turn into a five-star king
as a rat into a coachman.

She donated her dance card, fancy
slippers, fine china, and cedar chest
to Goodwill. Applied for—
and was hired as—the overseer

of kingdom operations. Daily
she ascends and descends the palace steps
wearing handmade, finely stitched,
soft leather boots fit for a king.

Note I Pinned to a Tree for Red Riding Hood's Mother
at the Edge of the Woods Where She Will Be Sure to Find It

My mother told me not to write.
She said I would hurt your feelings.
Your feelings should be hurt for sending
your daughter out into the woods with only
a bottle of wine, a cake, and
                                        innocence.
At least David had a slingshot.

Red Riding Hood should have known
that the woods are full of flowers and wolves,
that woodcutters don't just happen to be
in the right place with nothing better to do
than listen to how a grandmother is breathing.
It was up to you to tell her about Superman
and how he used his cloak. About foxes
in the henhouse. You should have
told her about Sappho and Earhart,
Roosevelt and Jong and how to depend
                                        on her intuition.
Red Riding Hood should have carried a list
of people to call and Nikes
                            a whistle
                            a black cat
                            a raven's mask.

She should have known karate
and how to feed that wolf the cake, wine—
then hit him over the head with the empty bottle.

The lesson wasn't that she should never again
wander off into the forest as long as she lived
but what my mother told me:
Always be polite but never dumb.

A grandmother isn't always what she seems.
A wolf is always a wolf.
The woods are full of flowers—
know when to stop and pick 'em.

Why Didn't the Princess's Mother
Tell the King to Stick It Up His Kingdom?

He was some kind of king
        alright
making his daughter keep her promise
taking in that ugly frog
        to sit by her plate
        drink from her cup
        run the length of her bed
leaving his spots

Frog knew a virgin when he caught one

The queen knew
        she hadn't taught
        her daughter not
to be afraid
of anything pointed

and the king knew a frog
        is a frog is
a hand to take up the reins of the kingdom

As for the princess
already she was compromised
ignorant as she was
        of open fields
        and choices

She didn't know she could hold
        the moon
        or a rose
        or absolutely nothing
between her fingers
and her thighs

She didn't know her body
        was a well
and one lost ball
didn't matter
one damn bit

Feather Leaf Tree

We had feathered many fowl
before we came to this:
pillows for the wizard's head.
Crafty bastard, he'd met no match
until this wily maiden learned
from her sisters' fates before her.
Wizard, she said, be damned.

When you're a feather you learn
the lay of the land.
We knew we'd never soften her head
in the wizard's marriage bed.
We knew by her nakedness.
We knew by the honey in her bath.

The taste of flight again was sweet.
We stuck to her close, shiny as leaves
after a rain to cover our lady's lie.
We remembered Icarus and easy
as a puff of innocence, we found
our way by the moon out of the kingdom.

She stripped us from her limbs, buried
us where the stream forks
at the forest's edge. There we sprout
burgundy flowers scented
like our lady's perfume, our bark
translucent as her skin,
our limbs high, remembering.

Tree Temple

Let us gather.

1.
We were in the garden,
of course, that first
garden without earthquakes
and moles, no fallen limbs or mold.

2.
Oh, we survived, celery-green
leaves tipped mandarin red
fanning the air filled with belches

and the princess
of the kingdom giving us away
as tokens, oh, the power

and the glory of cockroaches
and ferns, surviving the dinosaurs
as the world turns

3.
A veil weaves us.
The King and Guinevere
are in their castle,
Sir Lancelot off
somewhere, and the Round Table
as anything made
of wood
waits
       for the axe
       for the fire
       for rotting or wind.

We stay true to our flesh.

Take our pages, weave
your stories
while someone believes in the grail
and the cobwebs thrum.

We would never beg you come
into the unknown.

4.
We are a choir
of bones in winter.

There is the violin
the table
and this side of the wind
brushes Merlin's hand.

    Call in the animals.
    Call for the birds.
    Call down the mosses.

Let us begin.

5.
We grow hard
but graceful
our leaves glossy
thick.

That doesn't save
us from peeling.
Long thin strips
of our sunburned skin
slither like snakes

across the ground
our trunks cream-smooth,
naked.

6.
We saw Tommy snatch the fruit, forgetting
the story of Peter
in Mr. McGregor's garden.
We saw him offer the girl half
before she ran, until bulldozers scraped
the land, and we tasted like cardboard.

7.
Escher had us flame
upside down.

Under two
white leaves

carp grow
black moons

sounding
like doves.

They finger
the darker sky.

8.
Axe or saw
gallows or cross
we wept.

9.
And some night
we will tell you

how the nighthawk sings
how a butterfly sleeps
on the temple bell.

Aum.

III — LEAVINGS

Six pushes to New York by train after my mother married
my stepfather.
That train with its one bright eye, me in the dining room
looking out
at the backs of towns, eating French onion soup, then the
sun setting.
Darkness outside, dinner over. The start of my new
direction

cross-country to the rim of the Pacific where I ate oysters
on the half shell and fiddlehead ferns. Learned to be a
mother.
And while my children and I waited behind the crossing
gates
we sang: *Down at the station...Puff, puff, toot, toot/Off we go.*

We waved at the conductor in the caboose, went on down
the road.
For weeks we'd read *The Little Engine that Could.* But soon
like the caboose that years later would never follow an
engine
again—my children moved on. Others, too, like our lawyer

who slipped away from his caretaker in Kent, where trains
went zinging through town all hours; walked
under the streetlights to the tracks and stood on the rails,
the train's one bright eye with its gauges, valves,

and gearboxes coming faster faster—the engineer
having to live the rest of his life remembering.
Clickety-clack, clickety-clack, don't look back at where
we might have gone, might be instead.

Crossings

are hard.
Over a railroad track headed for
a funeral.
Over a river on a bridge
if
you're afraid of bridges
and heights. And water.
If
a bathtub is safe enough
but a river is not;
if the roads are flat
like brushstrokes in Illinois and Ohio
but not the Grand Tetons
and Olympics;
if
rice and oatmeal are easy to swallow
but oysters and jerky leave you gagging
and love with sweet kisses
is cool
but not the snoring
and stinky feet;
if
milkweed with its juice
and umbellate flowers is complicated
enough for you;
but the Milky Way with all
its individual stars, clusters, and bright
and dark nebulosities
is too much to
handle
then, whether
you believe in heaven or hell or not
believe that all
burials are hard to cross.

The Way I Came Out of the Cellar

My father fired the gun in his head.
My mother wouldn't let me see
the blood that day before Easter.
The dog howled with the siren.

My mother wouldn't let me see
my sister after she filled the garage
with car exhaust. Siren howled like a dog.
The funeral home smelled sickly sweet.

After my sister died in the garage
I moved from Ohio to Chicago
away from anything smelling sickly sweet.
I needed cold to clear my head.

I moved from Ohio to Chicago
but only for a few days.
I had needed wind and cold
but not such a furious wind.

From Chicago I went to the Pacific
quieted my guilt in the salt air
until I didn't see my father
fire the gun in his head.

Saving

My grandmother tried but wool sweaters
and crocheted cases disintegrated
in the wash after the mice and moths.

Bartenders took their turn, Schindler with his list
and King his marches, truth reaching like orchids,
their swollen roots forsaking the ground.

Song sparrows raise their hatchlings
in the shade of dying leaves, rainforests falling.
If only photographs were enough.

If only there were enough blood donors,
enough vaccines and rice. The gin pours clear.
The rat snakes are finding the bird eggs.

Finding My Grandmother's Childhood Home,
Öskü, Hungary

The old woman goes grave to grave
under shawl, apron,
babushka on a hot
August afternoon.
Tin watering can
holds her lopsided
among the wilted
daisies, sky ripped
open by jets. Horses
clip-clop the cobblestones,
wagons piled with hay,
air filled with the drone
of bees. She rises with dried
leaves swept from the plot,
points to a thatched house,
stoops again. Sun-hot
weeds stir in a poof
of breeze in the ditch
by the graves: Zozsef,
Nagy, Tomaskovics.

My Cinderella Story

Always a café
or diner along the way
even on a back

Maryland road.
I'd taken off my pink hat
with a veil the color

of DC's cherry blossoms.
Dick took off his tie.
This is the man who—

on our first date
six months back—fished the shoe
that had dropped off my foot

out of the ditch. We'd
eloped, married just hours
ago. Waiting for

our food, he put
a quarter in the slot machine
by the door. Coins

fell—a silver waterfall
out of the machine's mouth—
more than enough

to pay for our wedding
dinner. Days later
as we waited for

a ferry for home,
we ate the cake—frosting
hard as thick white cardboard,

the cake inside moist,
delicious. No forks, we ate
with our fingers.

Miscarriage

One month I hold
words like trust and future.

My heart is full, opening
and closing in time

to a tiny heart I can
almost hear. I had crossed over

from a place where dirty laundry
was never aired into this new state

of becoming, of begetting.
And now I'm sopping up blood.

I'm rocking silence.

Land of Alkali and Chromate

Erie with its dead fish in the '50s, the Cuyahoga River
burned. Air filled with chartreuse
particles and the earth wore a witch's lip around ponds
of sulfur, salt, a burbling black, gray, and yellow soup
waiting for my father to fall into.

He had grabbed at the slippery sides in the dark, muck
sucking his shoes off. When he finally
crawled out, his clothes were set like concrete.
The doctor said, *Being drunk*
probably saved him.

Today the river's clean. Erie's got herons and fish.
Diamond Alkali's been turned into high-ceilinged
apartments. And the Chromate's been razed
by men in protective clothing. The land lies
under new grass, fenced.

It will take a hundred years for the ground
to grow clean. Across the railroad tracks,
weeds grow around the headstones.

Having Been Born in Painesville

it's safe to say
that had I stayed   I would have died there.
            Days would have been punctuated
with agitation, juxtaposed with popsicles
from the ice cream truck.
            We were a culture of foragers.
Days would have meant creating fiction
filled with keys and compasses
interspersed with trips to the dump with my uncle
where every one of my senses was on edge
where rats were rats
burning wood was burning wood
and rubber tires smoldered.
            We were a culture of immigrants
            foraging in a new country.
Had I stayed, I would not
have found Dostoevsky or Woolf, never gone
to a concert or seen Picasso's
The Pomegranate Tree.
            I would have been a balloon
punctured with a needle, bagged
and ready for the dump.

Canned Peaches

My four-foot-eight grandmother toted
her eight-foot ladder and picked the fruit
without bruising. She left the plump suns
in the boiling water just long enough
to ease them out of their skins, then
pitted, peeled, and slurped each one
into the scalded jars of sugar water.
After the lids popped in their steam bath,
she stacked them like golden coins down
in the fruit cellar—their glowing halves
ready for the china bowls on Christmas
and the long snow-filled days after.

These days the winters in Ohio are warming.
Lake Erie isn't freezing. No one cans peaches.

Written Affair

My white cat surprises
a jay, so much blue
for one cat.
Fellow jays shake the leaves
of the maples and ash
with their squawking,
but they can't savor
the crunch of claws and beak.

Passion that leaked last night
onto the back seat
of a lover's car crusts
my buttocks. Carefully I wash
behind my ears as mother taught.
I douche. I think of lost
words, how we're known
by the company we keep
and what we can't give away.

Empty pages wait like the cat
to win, and I want to scrape
it all back, that passion
I could have spent
on words. Carefully I watch.
Will her fur turn blue?

General Note Written to Anyone Who Might Chance to
Discover One of My Lost Tupperware Bowls, That Stage of
My Life Happening to Be Over

Sloping sides keep turkey gizzards, hard-boiled eggs,
buttons, or screws—a bowl for every need priced to last
forever. Women wait to be taken into that middle-class
circle. What about loss, you ask?

I'm glad you asked. Just today I found one under the sink—
not quite like finding a Stegosaurus leg bone. But past
habits remind us how far we've come, how versatile.
For instance, I use the small pink bowl with its melted rim
on fish-cleaning days. Sometimes the fish leaps into
the sink. Such a satisfying rescue.

Children, I could ask, where did you hide them, pie
containers and popsicle molds? After tadpoles and the
garter snake minding its business under the quince,
where did they go. Friends, check your cupboards.
Lost friends, the ones I don't hear from at Christmas
anymore, let's get together.

And lovers, imagine opening something closed for six or
twenty years, mold grown that long in secret brought to
light. Tupperware like pink and yellow time capsules
keeping tight as lips... Think twice before breaking the seal.

Semi-Sonata of Oranges

1.
For days my grandmother circled the fruit with tiny craters
between her fingers before she opened the rind, stacked the
slivers like gold bills on the windowsill. She held the first
segment, a cache of sun like a prayer to her lips—better
than Christ's body or blood if she dared to tell—and
tongued its casing. First bite, her throat contracted
with its acid sweetness.

2.
Prokofiev left Russia and its revolution to feed his art—
Piano Concerto No. 3 and *Love for Three Oranges*. Oh,
the dissonance, enough to shake the fetters loose.
Lyrical beauty filled the vacant arms of men and women,
the notes suspended, holding themselves. Snow fell,
curtain dropped.

3.
A metaphor, I said, each Christmas as I tucked an orange in
my children's stockings, remembering my Gram's mustache
dancing above her lips as she talked
about walking to school in the snow wearing newspapers
in her shoes. That was on another continent in another life.
In my life with a jumble of tricycles, cameras, and books,
the oranges rotted in the stockings. Tradition didn't matter,
they said. Until the year Santa forgot.

4.
Cold snaps the life of orange trees in Florida, Florence,
Juneau. There's a run on the bins at Safeway, grown-ups
elbowing each other for the last orange globes, those acid-
sweet suns.

Original Sin on the Road

Doctrine told me I was born with it.
Priest said the same.
Landlocked, I couldn't see.

Scripture explained why
forgiveness was born. A carrot
litanized to keep us. *Yay though...*

always that damn valley to walk through.
My heart was heavy as an engine
in a '41 Ford. The more miles

I put on, the more language grew,
dictionaries and novels full of
delicious, adventitious, sensual want.

I found God had wanted, not Mary.
My breasts swelled, my heart raced
to keep up. I bought a one-owner

Chevy, and mine was a kingdom
on its own now, me at the wheel
driving back roads and freeways

through blizzards and tornadoes, flat
plains and mountains into Death Valley
where I stopped.

Ordered that hitchhiker named naysayer
out. Floored the pedal for my meeting
in San Francisco with the sea.

The Yolk and the White of It

It is, inside the egg
shades of an old wedding dress
pale light rounded
and virgin
unscented yet
by barnyard.

Still, in there
surrounded by feathers and straw
sounds of coyote and boy
who caught his hand in the combine
waiting
like the hawk's wing laying its shadow
or fingers taking their turn
nest, basket, rim
of the fry pan.

On the other hand, could be
an inside job—lightning strike
of the egg tooth
and open ever after
to foxes, cocks,
and axes that fix
Sunday dinners.

This is the lesson
of leaving what's fragile
behind.

IV — AFTER

I wake to trains in the Green River Valley at the foot
of an active volcano. My heart had been fine, pumping
steady
for years until one night it erupted into A-fib—my bed
shaking
like a motel bed that had been fed a quarter in the '50s—

my heart somersaulting between 33 and 188 beats. The red
truck.
Hospital. Pads in case they had to shock me back. With
bleeping
monitors as chorus, I had this epiphany: my heart is an
engine—
the locomotive of my body without wheels.

I said, *I'm not ready to go.* I still want 10 pushes on that
glider—
a plane trip across the ocean where I'll step aboard
the Venice Simplon-Orient-Express, the train that Hercule
Poirot rode
as he sipped crème de menthe. Maybe I'll sip
a Manhattan.

Wolf, I Remember You

First with the pigs. Bad wolf.
Red Riding Hood, of course.

Bad wolf.

But wolf you were the wild
I'd hid from myself.

Wolf, you were kin.
Wolf, you howled in my dreams.

Art of Conjugating *To Desire*

> *There is no end / to desire*
> —William Carlos Williams

In my house filled with its hidden stories,
the kite tied to my wrist knows the scent of the sea.

My house with three storeys of secrets groans
like the wooden hull of a ship. I take down

the numbered boxes—each month a new view—
sunset, tulip field, lake, or mountain. I knew

flatland, ditches, and ponds. Now I want to climb
an active volcano, stand on a thousand times

a thousand years of ice, bite my ice axe
into the glacier on the edge of a crevasse

so deep it's purple. I want to wade waves
that roll in like a mantra, a month of Sundays,

sails of my ship full, sunset threaded by my bow—
and good weather ahead, I pray, not foul.

Rainier

This is the mountain where blizzards can convince you
there is or is not a god.
This is the mountain I did not summit.

This is the mountain where fire-eating dragons live in ice
    caves.
It's been foretold that an eruption will send rivers in new
    directions
and wipe out hills and valleys all the way to Puget Sound.

This is the mountain where I left Paradise Inn with other
    climbers.
When we left Camp Muir the next morning, I heard ice
    melting. A storm
was coming in; at 12,000 feet the guide turned three of us
    back.

This is the mountain where there is no absence because
    direction
is only how close the chasm might be—

                           a deep dark
                          purple mouth
                          as I slipped
                          as I gouged my axe
                          into the ice
                          that would not hold.

This is where god danced with me on the edge of the world
where a rope and three young climbers with their ice axes
stopped our fall.

This is the mountain where I made it back to Paradise,
kneeled and kissed the parking lot, prayed

that the dragons in that mountain wouldn't wake
until after I made it down to sea level and home.

Altars

Once I knew the grain of the altar
>   as I sat on hardwood pews under the cross
>   God's word *a lamp unto my feet.*

Then I stopped believing
>   in God's son and his father, forgot the altar
>   with its cloth washed, ironed by the faithful

forgot about the plate of crackers
>   and cup of wine, the priest robed in black
>   with a white collar and dominion over all.

Now I build altars
>   out of shells, stones, flowers, and a crow feather
>   that had fallen at my feet.

The Ten Stations of Worship

This is the hand held for safety's sake,
palms raised to show the most traveled paths.

This is the foot, bunioned and mud-stained—
Russian steppes, ice caves, olive groves.

This is the leg, striding or curved, lotus-like
in the California poppies.

This is the eye seeing curled ferns and symbols.
This is the eye of permission. Amen.

This is the lap, a nest reminiscent of goose down.
We've learned to fold, to wait.

This is the breast we come to and come to—
our need for suckle, beauty, forgiveness, grace.

This is the vagina, seedpod moist
with its own rain.

This is the truth of fecundity.
Of creating. Birth.

This is the other mouth
we depend on—the telling and retelling

of old tales, fables, myths, and healing.
In a temple of trees, we say *Yes*.

Afternoon Affair

In an arroyo
wind stirs

the heather and flox
lifts my nipples

brushes my lips
and this rush

like sunlighted
water spills

through a fissure
in the land.

Eight Notes to Some of You Who Make Me Happy

> Dear Garlic,
>
> Louis Diat said: *Without garlic I simply would not care to live.*
>
> Someone else said that communion and sex are about the only things that don't go well with garlic.
>
> I disagree. You, garlic, go with anything.
>
> I agree with my grandmother: You ward off evil. She put you in soup, goulash, and put a thread through a clove to tie around my neck if I felt a cold coming on.
>
> I rode with a man to another state and married him. Of course, he cooked with garlic.

Artichokes,

the two of you, knobby-headed,
wait in my crisper for the knife
the pot, and water, olive oil
for the steam to soften your hearts.

My heart has turned to rock
or mush, I can't tell which.
I don't want to get out of bed.

All I know is that the two of you
are going to rot unless I rise, peel
your leaves one at a time until
I reach your hearts, smear them
with mayonnaise. Eat. And after?

I'll remember when two of us
shared one of you with candles
and shots of tequila in bed.

Cabbage

You've been called dense
without pretense

the common man's lettuce
related to radish

and rutabaga
full of bulk and vigor

good for turkeys and swine.
From prehistoric times

you've grown over
yourselves: sea otter's

Chinese, St. Patrick's
as if you had secrets.

Indeed, masters of the folding
arts, indigenous and long

lasting, older than taxes,
almost older than sex,

you've kept the earth's pulse,
purging wounds full of pus.

Montaigne wanted death
to find him in his garden

with his cabbages. You're here
and *the earth exhales.*

Oh, My Beloved Potatoes,

You push without legs, like cocoons
the color of maggots inveigling
your way past pill bugs, worms,
antennae reaching for the feel
of rain, not just wetness but for
the music of it, by now your eyes
opened, unfurling. You lie
like a memory, waiting for the spade.
You keep your nightshade
family to yourselves, pockets growing
among the soil and millipedes, stones
singing their own stories of kingdoms
and uprisings, the potato-eaters, miners
and stone masons, all of them knowing
      by the sweat of their brows.

Hello, Cheetos

I had you all to myself once—
no sisters sharing, a whole bag
filled with what my grandmother
would never have fed me.
Even your name—like "cheery o"
those *e*'s and that *o* rolling
off my tongue, my mind colored
comic-book neon orange
like all things magic—circuses,
Superman, Wonder Woman, and jazz.
Let's make another date, Cheetos, for
our Friday night alone.

Pomegranate,

Chang Ch'ien brought you, symbol
of a womb filled with children,
from the Middle East to China.

Rubens painted *The Fall of Man*—
Eve eating not an apple but the seeds
of your thick-skinned fruit.

Here on the rim of the Pacific, I hold
one of your daughters in my palm,
ripe and heavy.

When I cut, her blood runs
through my fingers and I guide her shiny
red pearls into a blue bowl—

You, pomegranate, born in Eve's garden—
                her hand reaching
                her hunger sharp.

To You, Oysters, That Gave Me 12 Ways to Pray

One oyster.
Two oysters.
Three oysters. Four.

      I wade into Willapa Bay
      through the ooze
      and turn of the bay

           oysters, clams, gulls, herons
           and the suck of my boots
           in this living bay at the northern end
           of the Peninsula.

Five oysters.
Six oysters. Seven.

      Unity of Earth's Four Corners,
      completeness, and the number
      of vertebrae in my spine.

           Eight. Nine
           of you open and shut in response
           to the moon's pull, tides
           driven by a dead rock.

Magic 12.

      A cardinal number.
      Sun risen each day in 12 months.

           Shucked, you wait
           in a circle just for me,
           sun setting over the bay.

I take.
I eat.
I drink the sea of you—coppery, briny, sweet.

Meditation with Peach

I run
through raindrops
from the fruit stand
to my car

rain
sluices
the windows
baptizes the roof

each bite
wholly for myself

my shoulders rise
into the clouds

with each inhale
thoughts fall
away
like a river down
streaming
to the sea

each swallow

each
blessed
bite

each breath
in/out

Bindweed

I know there is a flutter in my heart
this pain in my knee
and a thousand or more leaves
in the oak's canopy. All true
at the same time. My mother
is dead, but she's there in the photo
of my new garden. Sunflowers, sage.
Now my garden is mossed-over
bindweed holding the rotted bench
in place. Poppies and lilies of the valley
gone. Only a few tulips in resurrection.
All at once but not at the same time.

Time is not the same as all at once.
Gone except for a few tulips resurrected.
No poppies and lilies of the valley.
Bindweed holds the rotted bench
my garden now mossed over.
My garden of sunflowers and sage
dead. But she's there in the photo
at the same time—my mother
under the oak's canopy, true
as the thousand or more leaves at the same time
just as there is this pain in my knee
a flutter called A-fib in my heart.

Places That Made Me

Poverty Bay/   the Russian Pale of Settlement/

Des Moines Food Bank/   Wolf Haven/

Copper Canyon/   Sunday School's heaven and hell/

Shangri-la/   Makgadikgadi Salt Pans/   semicircle

of flames and Tibetan prayer flags at Qutuo Pass/

bottle of gin/   Painesville garbage dump with its rats/

Spot Tavern with a jukebox full of blues/   college

classroom for sex/ my mother's funeral/   pickled

pigs' feet/ 50 years of marriage/ Walla Walla State

Penitentiary/   park bench I called home/ Cuyahoga River

burning/   Moonstone Beach with driftwood, dead gull

and knife-sharp grasses that can cut an eye/   Museum

of Mummies/   manufacturing plant of mistakes/

Willapa Bay oyster beds/   Chromate's soup ponds/

my father's murder and sister's suicide/   cry of a loon/

trail out of a dark woods/   yesterday

Recipe for Making a Day

I sip my coffee with a few cashews
and apricots. Joy Harjo says
the world begins at the kitchen table.
I thank those who have cooked for me.
Think about that first brave soul who ate
an artichoke. A pomegranate. Oyster.

Lots of leafy greens for lunch paired
with tomatoes, black beans, and avocado.
I write a love poem using the words *spheres*
and *Nirvana*. Plan a celebration of *p*'s
for the week: peaches, persimmons, pears,
pomegranates, pepitas, and peas, and watch

a slug enjoying one of my lettuce leaves.
This leads me to clear a trail through my forest
of worries. I'm Zen-like. *Chop wood. Carry water.*
Once a lover of baseball, I repeat: *Build it*
and they will come. I decide on oysters
or salmon for dinner. Depend on my intuition.

Two Letters

1.
To My Martian and Hungarian Ancestors

I do not yearn for Mars. Do not aspire to go back.
I have adjusted to earth's tether and songs of the season.

I have fancied myself a bird above the graves
of all you before me, you an ambidextrous people
breathing music and math.

I did not inherit a brain for numbers.
I am not musical, but I pen words on a page
and they have their own rhythm.

I knew rivers and lakes and hills in Ohio. But I wanted
mountains and the sea.

Bartók wrote that *the body (its matter) is eternal; the soul
(the form of the body) is transitory.* I believe that the only
immortal part of humans are the atoms
that make up our bodies.

I traced Euclid's theory and decided prime numbers
are pinpricks of light falling without sound.

Sound is everywhere in the inner altar's great stones
                blessed by Neptune and Jupiter,
                by spider, grapevines, lightning.
                I hear their birthings

throbbing with that blue planetary hum.

2.
Reminders to Self

Remember the stories. Face east.
Remember the lessons of gravity
and what you sow you reap.

> Keep a vase of petunias
> on the windowsill.

Face west with its deep dark waters
that talk the language of waves. Each
translation carries the translator's stamp.

> Revel in the sounds of Bach, Aretha,
> and Satchmo.

Face north and picture lightning,
the Northern Lights, planets, stars.
Energy changes form but isn't lost.

> Hang a wreath of vines
> on the door.

Face south over willows, birches, pines.
Praise the work of the world growing
under the topsoil. Don't mess your nest.

> Light a candle
> on the kitchen table.

Each morning honor what you see.
Seek to see what you can't.
Ask a blessing on your body, your house.
Listen.

NOTES

Poems appearing on the title pages of Section I through IV are the four parts of a long poem titled "Trains."

Painesville, Ohio
According to the City of Painesville's website, the city was settled in 1800. Painesville is the county seat of Lake County, Ohio, located along the Grand River, roughly 30 miles northeast of Cleveland and 2.5 miles from the shores of Lake Erie. Painesville is home to Lake Erie College and Morley Library. The city is named after General Edward Paine who served in the Revolutionary War and settled in the area shortly after.

There were two main chemical companies in Painesville when I was growing up—the Diamond Alkali Company and the Diamond Shamrock Chromate plant. My mother, birth father, and stepfather worked at the Diamond. My uncle worked at the Chromate. The area contained "soup ponds"—chemical settling basins that included chromium, coke tar, hydrogen, magnesium, sodium hydroxide, and a number of other toxic chemicals and hazardous waste. "...The study found people who worked at the Diamond Shamrock chromate plant in Painesville Township were 15 to 29 times more likely to die of lung cancer than the county's general population...." You can read more at pressbooks.ulib.csuohio.edu/from-across-the-pond-palmond Chapter 11. Cleveland, 1979 – From Across the Pond

In the first poem, section subtitled "Sunflowers": Béla Viktor János Bartók (1881–1945) was a Hungarian composer, pianist, and ethnomusicologist. He is considered one of the most important composers of the 20th century; he and Franz Liszt are regarded as Hungary's greatest composers. Through his collection and analytical study of folk music, he was one of the founders of comparative musicology, which later became known as ethnomusicology. (Wikipedia)

I also use the quote where common revolutionaries take action by Isaac Breuer, 1883–1946. Breuer was a rabbi in the German Neo-Orthodoxy movement. He was born in Pápa, Austria-Hungary. Austria-Hungary is often referred to as the Austro-Hungarian Empire or the Dual Monarchy. It was a multinational constitutional monarchy in Central Europe between 1867 and 1918. Austria-Hungary was a military and diplomatic alliance of two sovereign states with a single monarch. (Wikipedia)

Pápa is the same town my grandfather (my mother's father) was born in. His last name was Magar, which changed to Mogar after he came to America. My grandmother's last name before she came to America was Tomaskovics, which was changed to Thomas.

In the first poem, third section:
I use a quote from Meister Eckhart (born c. 1260, died 1327/28? in Avignon, France). He was a Dominican theologian and writer considered to be the greatest German speculative mystic. In the transcripts of his sermons in German and Latin, he charts the course of union between the individual soul and God. (*Britannica*)

...all the king's horses and all the king's men is from the nursery rhyme "Humpty Dumpty sat on a wall," probably originally a riddle and one of the best known in the English-speaking world. (Wikipedia)

"Old Shoe Woman Who Wasn't There in the 1930s Print" refers to a nursery rhyme, "There was an old woman who lived in a shoe." The earliest printed version comes from Joseph Ritson's *Gammer Gurton's Garland* in 1784. Ritson is known today for editing the first academic collection of Robin Hood ballads. (abebooks.com)

"The Way I Came Out of the Cellar" is after Kim Addonizio's poem "Childhood."

Rainier
According to the official Mt. Rainier National Park website, Mt. Rainier ascends to 14,410 feet above sea level. It stands as an icon in the Washington State landscape. An active volcano, Mount Rainier is the most glaciated peak in the contiguous USA, spawning five major rivers. Subalpine wildflower meadows ring the icy volcano while ancient forest cloaks Mount Rainier's lower slopes. Wildlife abounds in the park's ecosystems.

Mt. Rainier's indigenous name is Tahoma.

I made it to 12,000 plus feet and did not attempt to climb again.

ACKNOWLEDGEMENTS

I am grateful to the following journals and presses that published the following poems, some revised and with different titles:

CALYX: A Journal of Art and Literature by Women: "Under Heaven"

Empty Bowl Bress, *Madrona Cookbook*: "My Grandmother's Hungarian Horns and Sunday Dinner"

Last Leaves Magazine: "Canned Peaches"

The Meadow Photo 2: "The house built out of a chicken coop sits in a field"

New River Review Photo 1: "no names on the back, only the black and white"

Nimrod International Journal of Poetry: "Bindweed"

Other Voices: "Bleach," "Cabbage," "Feather Leaf Tree," "Oh, Potatoes," "Rampion, the Beautiful," and "Tree Temple"

"Tree Temple" was first "published" in collaboration with Art Wolfe's paintings at the Frye Art Museum, Seattle

Papeachu Press and *Of Our Own Accord*: "Miscarriage"

The Poetry Box, *Journey of Trees*: "The Ten Stations of Worship"

Ravena Press, *Triple #17*: "Crossings"

Seattle Arts: "Note I Pinned to a Tree for Red Riding Hood's Mother at the Edge of the Woods where She Will Be Sure to Find It"

The Small Pond Magazine of Literature: "The Yolk and the White of It"

The Sow's Ear and *What We Bury Changes the Ground*: "Why Some Hungarians Dream Equations and Notes"

The Spoon River Poetry Review: "Written Affair"

SWWIM: "Afternoon Affair"

Syracuse Cultural Workers 2025 Datebook: "Pomegranate"

Tebot Bach, *What We Bury Changes the Ground*: "Finding My Grandmother's Childhood Home, Öskü, Hungary," "Semi-Sonata of Oranges," and "The Cemetery Again"

"Land of Alkali and Chromate" was also published in *Pontoon*

"My Mother's Birth" was Part 3 of a longer poem titled "My Grandmother's Stories, Translated."

WomenArts Quarterly Journal: "Why Didn't the Princess's Mother Tell the King to Stick It Up His Kingdom?"

GRATITUDE

I know I will forget some people I should thank for this book. The list is long and I am grateful for the friends, fellow writers, teachers, and residencies that have given me friendship, critiques, and support.

Thank you:

Lana Hechtman Ayers of MoonPath Press for publishing this book—and all the other Northwest poets whose beautiful books you've published.

Centrum, Hedgebrook, Ragdale, Soapstone, The Flying Squirrel, Whiteley, Willapa Bay AiR (Artists in Residence), and Willard R. Espy for residencies.

John Davis, Sharon Hashimoto, Bob McNamara, Sati Mookherjee, Arlene Naganawa, Michael Spence, Ann Spiers, and John Willson—my long-time group of poets and friends.

My Third Tuesday group of friends: Kelli Russell Agodon, Chris Balk, Michele Bombardier, Katy E. Ellis, Susan Rich, and Cindy Veach.

A second shout-out to Michele Bombardier, my writing partner during and after Covid.

The EDGE group: Catalina Cantú, Ann Hursey, Gabriela Denise Frank, and Lynn Knight, who give me views into all the genres, not just poetry.

A second shout-out to Gabriela Denise Frank for her amazing cover art.

My memoir group: Mary Pat Griswold, Irene Hopkins, Ruth Marcus, and Heidi Seawall.

Connie Braun, Robin Davidson, Carolyn Forché, and Lisa Morano, who have been with me at Hedgebrook and to Greece and Paris and back.

And Kim Addonizio, Debby Bacharach, Karen Bjork, Scott Cairns, Caroline Cumming, Alice Deery, Suzanne Edison, Lynne Ellis, Elizabeth Falcon, Jennifer Franklin, Tess Gallagher, Ilya Kaminsky, Kaaren Kitchell, Sigrun Susan Lane, Sam Ligon, Gary Copeland Lilley, Corinne Mar, Kristie McLean, Nadine Ellsworth-Moran, Bill Ransom, Lois Rosen, Heidi Seaborn, Patricia Smith, Lillo Way, Carolyne Wright, Sandy Yannone.

ABOUT THE ARTIST

Gabriela Denise Frank is a transdisciplinary artist, editor, educator, and winner of the Fern Academy Prize. The author of the forthcoming fiction collection *How to Not Become the Breaking* (Gateway Literary Press, 2025), she serves as creative nonfiction editor of *Crab Creek Review*. www.gabrieladenisefrank.com

ABOUT THE AUTHOR

Susan Landgraf has published more than 400 poems in *Prairie Schooner, Poet Lore, Margie, Nimrod, Third Wednesday, SWWIM, CALYX, Rattle*, and others. Books include *Journey of Trees* published by The Poetry Box; *Crossings* published by Ravenna Press as part of its Triple series; *The Inspired Poet* from Two Sylvias Press; *What We Bury Changes the Ground* from Tebot Bach; *Other Voices* from Finishing Line Press; and *Student Reflection Journal for Student Success* published by Prentice Hall.

An Academy of American Poets Laureate award in 2020 resulted in a book of Muckleshoot Indian Tribe poetry titled *A Muckleshoot Poetry Anthology: At the Confluence of the Green and White Rivers* published by Washington State University Press in 2024.

Landgraf has given more than 150 workshops and readings in the US and abroad, including the Port Townsend Writers' Conference, San Miguel Writers' Conference, Marine and Science Technology Center, and Antioch International, Oxford, England. She is the recipient of a Theodore Morrison Scholarship for Bread Loaf and grants from Artist Trust, Jack Straw, and King County Arts Commission.

A former journalist, she taught at Highline College for 30 years and at Shanghai Jiao Tong University. She served as Poet Laureate of Auburn, Washington, from 2018 to 2020.

www.ingramcontent.com/pod-product-compliance
Lightning Source LLC
LaVergne TN
LVHW041617070526
838199LV00052B/3176